# WOMEN'S SOCCER:
# THE OFFICIAL HISTORY
# OF THE UNOFFICIAL
# WORLD CUPS

# FOREWORD

Did you know that a 15-year-old girl scored a hat-trick in the final of a World Cup in front of 110,000 people in Mexico? Or that prior to the formation of the United States Women's National Team in 1985, the country was successful represented in tournaments around the world by a club of young players from Texas? Well before the first ever official Women's World cup organised by FIFA in 1991, all sorts of unofficial tournaments were held around the world, in countries as far apart as Mexico, Italy, Japan and China.

While some were put together by money-grabbing businessmen and others by women looking to promote the cause of feminism, the "renegade" tournaments held in the 1970s and 1980s played a crucial role in the development of women's soccer. Without these competitions, women would likely never have got the chance to have a World Cup of their own officially recognized by FIFA at any point in the 20th century.

In addition to the pressure that they put on the international federation, the unofficial Women's World Cups were responsible for many an interesting – yet largely unknown – chapter in the history of women's football.

This book traces the exploits of the first world champion women's teams as well as the lengthy process that finally led to official recognition. It contains stories never before documented, combining politics, sporting prowess and anecdotes the like of which would be impossible to imagine in today's context. The following chapters will take you through the seminal tournaments and matches from the 1970s and 1980s courtesy of exclusive interviews with the players of the time, those pioneers of women's soccer who represented the likes of France, Canada, Italy and Belgium.

If France was able to host the Women's World Cup in 2019, it is thanks in no small part to the campaigning of a band of men and particularly women in the early 1990s. This book is about them – and what they achieved.

# HISTORY OF THE
# *COPPA DEL MONDO*
# OR *MUNDIAL*

T he world of soccer was not ready for women. It was a closed shop made up of men who took until 1991 to organize the first official Women's World Cup, 61 years after the inaugural men's version in Uruguay.

And while things did start to take shape between the late 1960s and the early 1970s, some of the archive material from that time shows that football was simply a reflection of the prevailing mind-set at the time. In an article in French daily newspaper *"Le Monde"* published on 5 November 1969, referring to the first unofficial Women's European Championship played in Italy that year, journalist Michel Castaing wondered about the ability of women to actually play soccer. *"It is a 'male' team sport... (representing man) in all that is most virile and athletic that is open to the people"*, he said, before continuing in what can only be described as a similar vein:

> *There were around 60 of them, in Aosta and Novara on Saturday, Turin on Sunday, swapping their silk stockings for woolen ones[...]A team of beautiful warriors, no doubt tired of washing the kit for their brother, boyfriend or husband, of trailing around after them at soccer stadiums them every week or having to watch it on television on*

*Sunday afternoons, but most of all wanting to show that women were indeed capable of kicking a ball of this kind. And much to our surprise, we are prepared to admit, they actually managed it.*

The article was entitled *"The women's 'soccer player' – a new breed of athlete makes it European bow in Turin"* and is available on line in the *"Le Monde"* archives. The words 'women's soccer player' appear in inverted commas, indicating the poor levels of credibility that they were accorded at the time. Not that the French press were the only ones guilty of not taking the sport seriously at the time. In a paper entitled *"The history of women's soccer in Europe from the Great War up to the present day"*, the author Xavier Breuil quotes from an article published in 1971 in a Swiss magazine. The journalist in question described going to a women's soccer match as *"like going to the circus or a women's wrestling contest"*.

It was against this background that the first women's team at French club Stade de Reims was formed in the summer of 1968 thanks to journalist and coach Pierre Geoffroy. In an excellent television report by Yvonne Debeaumarché called *"Les filles du stade"*, there is archive film in which the man who would go on to coach the French international women's team said that he was looking for *"an attraction for a type of annual fair that was held every year in Reims"*. While the attraction chosen for 1968 was indeed a women's soccer match, the report informs us that the previous year's entertainment was a midget wrestling bout...

The idea of entertainment combined with the somewhat unhealthy curiosity that soccer played by women engendered, putting them more or less in the same category as circus animals, was something that certain people managed to turn into a profit. Between the late 1960s and the early 1970s, a number of Italian businessmen – who were behind the aforementioned unofficial women's European championship – made attempts to promote the sport for commercial gain.

They were joined in their efforts by other entrepreneurs of varying degrees of trustworthiness, and together they formed the International and European Women's Football Association (FIEFF), whose main members had absolutely no affiliation with the world of soccer. The president, by the name of Dr. Lucci, was a legal professional, while the vice-president was also an attorney, and indeed most of the advisers were businessmen from the executive board of *Martini & Rossi* who financed the majority of the unofficial tournaments that followed.

This was the context in which FIEFF organized in 1970 –in Italy, of course – the first *Coppa del Mondo*, also called the *Martini Rosso Cup*, featuring eight teams. While the tournament was considered a success for the organizers, with the final between Italy and Denmark apparently watched by 40,000 spectators, the FIEFF representatives from other countries were less impressed, and rightly so. It transpired that in order to maximize income, the Italian businessmen had quite simply rigged the draw so that the host country would meet the best European team at the time in the final, namely Denmark. The draw initially had Italy and Denmark slated to meet in the semi-final, and so they ignored that and tried again... The second draw had the desired effect, with the two preferred teams meeting in the final, which Denmark won 2-0.

On the back of the success of the first *Coppa del Mondo*, the Italian opportunists looked to organize a second tournament the following year, but the scandals of the inaugural version and the thinly-veiled overtly commercial intentions of the organizers led to various federations from other countries consulting FIFA then turning down the offer to take part. FIFA naturally supported the decision of those who chose to stay away, as this press release illustrates:

*If you consult a list of representatives of women's football across the various countries, you will immediately realize that they are unknown in footballing circles in their own countries, and instead are managers and agents of companies with advertising capacity or who are merely trying to make money by exploiting football played by women as a 'show'.*

Despite this warning from FIFA, six teams nevertheless took part in the second *Coppa del Mondo* in Mexico in 1971, namely the host country, France, Italy, Denmark, England and Argentina. This competition would prove to be a huge success. Local television broadcast the matches and thousands of supporters flocked to the stadiums to watch the action and get autographs from the players after the final whistle. Alas, business and profits were once again allowed to take priority over the sporting aspects. The organizers were keen to fill their pockets and did everything in their power to ensure that host country Mexico would meet world champions Denmark in the final. The draw for the groups was (once again) rigged and the Mexico .v. Italy semi-final saw a comedy of refereeing errors inflicted on the Squadra Azzurra.. The Italians also claimed that on the eve of the match, Mexican fans spent the entire night making a cacophony of noise outside their hotel to prevent them from sleeping! There is of course no proof that the perpetrators were sent by the tournament organizers (or indeed that they were not...)

This further interference saw FIEFF lose any trust they still had from the other countries. FIFA and UEFA strongly advised any national associations that had authorized women's soccer in their country against taking part in non-approved competitions or ones organized by that particular body. Having lost its credibility and been made persona non grata by the two main governing bodies of the sport, FIEFF did not manage to convince any teams to participate in a third *Coppa del Mondo* in 1972, and the federation was duly dissolved that year.

FIEFF should not be seen as the root of all evil in women's soccer terms, however. It was highly likely that the lure of financial gain and not passion for the sport was the driving force behind the Italian businessmen who ran the federation. However, from 1968 to 1972 (both as the FICF – *Federazione Italiana de calcio femminile* –

and then from 1970 as FIEFF after changing its name), these entrepreneurs organized three major competitions: a European championship in 1969 and two World Cups in 1970 and 1971. These tournaments enabled women to create awareness in the corridors of FIFA, UEFA and various other national soccer federations, and to showcase their talent. This was particularly the case at the second *Coppa del Mondo* (which in the host country was known as the *Campeonato mundial de futbol femenil* or quite simply the *Mundial*) in Mexico in 1971. That tournament has faded into the mists of time, but it deserves a prominent place in any catalogue of the history of soccer, men's or women's.

# MEXICO 71

## II CAMPEONATO MUNDIAL DE FUTBOL FEMENIL

# xochitl

## boletín 1

# MUNDIAL 1971

**Venue**: Mexico

**Organized by**: The International and European Women's Football Federation (FIEFF)

**Date**: 15 August – 5 September 1971

I n the early 1970s, women's soccer still trailed a long way behind the men's version as far as national associations and international federations were concerned. An illustration of this is the fact that the second *Coppa del Mondo* - or *Mundial* –was held in August and September 1971, over a year after Pele had taken Mexico by storm. By then, it was far too late for the women to ride the men's coat-tails – the fan and media interest generated by the ninth men's World Cup organized by FIFA was long gone. By the summer of 1971, Pele was a long way away from Mexico, and even further from imagining that a 15-year-old could be capable of making history in her sport...

"*My parents discussed whether they should let me go to Mexico or not,*" explained Susanne Augustesen, one of the Denmark players who was just 15 at the time. "*They had some persuading to do as far as my school was concerned as it meant missing a whole month of lessons.*" Once all of the money and study-related issues had been sorted out, Augustesen's parents agreed for her to travel all the way from her native Holbæk in Denmark and fly over to Mexico to play in an international competition – which was not something that they had been bargaining for... Between the rigged draws of the first tournament in 1970 and the warnings issued by the various international bodies governing soccer, the members of FIEFF struggled to convince the relevant national associations to let their teams take part. The qualifiers which were meant to decide which teams would get to play in the tournament in Mexico were a fiasco, with just five of the 13 expected teams participating. To save face, FIEFF used friendlies that had been played earlier in the year to allow certain countries to qualify and to eliminate others without anyone actually being aware of the process! Thus it was that Denmark qualified courtesy of a 4-0 win over Sweden in a friendly! *"I played in match against Sweden but I didn't know that it was a qualifier for the World Cup,"* a highly amused Augustesen recalled.

The Stade de Reims players had a similar reaction to their qualification for the *Mundial* after recording a win over the Netherlands in April 1971 in what was the French women's team's first official match. *"After the match, our coach Pierre Geoffroy told us that that victory would enable us to go and play in the World Cup in Mexico,"* former Reims player Colette Guyard explained. *"He hadn't told us any of this beforehand!"* The French Football Federation (FFF) had sent the Stade de Reims team plus a handful of other players from the neighboring Champagne region to play the match so as not to go against the recommendations issued by FIFA and UEFA, a fact confirmed in a letter dated February 1971 and signed by the director general of the FFF at the time, Michel Cagnion:

> *Based on the highly reticent attitude on a number of occasions shown by the European (football) Union towards competitions which are not under its control, (the FFF) is authorizing a team to take part under its own auspices at the first women's world championships.*

This was a crafty way of having France represented without sending a team under the aegis of the national technical directorate, and this is one of the reasons why many countries were represented by clubs at the various World Cups played in the 1970s and 1980s.

As was the case at the previous tournament, the main sponsor was the Italian firm *Martini & Rossi* who covered all the costs for the six teams who were invited, namely Mexico, France, Denmark, Argentina, Italy and England. All six countries were amazed upon their arrival at the airport in Mexico, in particular the English, who had 13-and-a-half-year-old Leah Caleb in their ranks. *"Photographers were there waiting for us,"* she said. *"Our bus couldn't get through the crowds. People were waving at us and applauding. It was totally surreal." "We were put up at a lovely hotel. We had a police escort wherever we went and we were signing autographs all the time,"* her team-mate Chris Lockwood added. Thanks to an efficient publicity campaign and wide-spread media coverage, the Mexican *Mundial* proved popular with the local. Some 80,000 people flocked to the Azteca Stadium on 15 August to watch the opening ceremony, which featured parades, military choirs, national anthems, the teams themselves, a speech from the vice-president of the FIEFF and a deluge of red, white and green balloons in the colors of the host nation... It was quite a party, and put the onus on the players to respond once they literally got the ball rolling...

With the aforementioned 80,000 spectators in the stands, the Mexicans kicked off the first match against their rivals from Argentina. Maria Eugenia Rubio opened the scoring for *la Tri,* as the host nation's women's team is affectionately known, in the 21st minute, with team-mate Patricia Hernandez doubling their advantage just a few minutes later. Argentina pulled one back before the break, which was the signal for the first of the half-time shows, which during the various matches of the tournament would feature dancers, entertainment and demonstrations of local sports such as pelota mixteca (a type of tennis played without a net). *"It was like a carnival,"* Lockwood said of the half-time festivities.

After the break in the opening match, Rubio bagged a second goal to seal victory for *la Verde* (another of their nicknames) 3-1. The defeat left a bitter taste in the mouth of the South Americans, however, who were convinced that they had been given unfair treatment by the officials. *"They were the host country, so Mexico had to make it through to the final,"* said Argentina's Marta Soler in an interview with the website *Pagina 12* in 2018. *"The referee disallowed a perfectly good goal. The match was an absolute scandal."* In light of the previous tournament, her claim hardly comes as a surprise...

It may not have sold out the 110,000-capacity Azteca Stadium, but it was still a remarkable achievement for an opening match, particularly since the tickets were not handed out free of charge. Face value was between 30 and 80 pesos (USD 1.50 – USD 3.50). To help the financial situation a little further, the organizers were keen to sell various items of tournament merchandise including t-shirts, badges, bags and even dolls of the official mascot Xochitl, a slim young girl with a soccer ball at her feet, wearing a Mexican team jersey and matching (very short) shorts. The exaggerated sexualization of the mascot is worth looking at in more detail.

Jaime de Haro, who was president of the organizing committee for the *Mundial,* made a frank admission before the tournament even began in a New York Times article dated 27 June 1971. *"We are going to focus on the femininity,"* he said, a decision which he saw as *"a natural one"* since *"soccer and women are two of the main passions of most men around the globe"*. The article continues with the journalist explaining that the players will have access to beauty salons in the locker rooms so that they can *"be interviewed and go to public ceremonies wearing false eyelashes, lip-stick and a pretty hair-style"*, before adding that the players' shorts would be as sexy as possible... With the article being written before the tournament began, there was no way for the *New York Times* journalist to know that things would not come to pass as he had described.

Based on the archive photographs and videos available, it is clear to see that the kit worn by the players during matches was far from skin-tight and alluring. While the shorts were certainly shorter than those worn by the women at the 2019 World Cup, those worn by Pele in 1970 were a lot shorter than those at the tournament in 2018. Certain archive images even show Denmark and Argentina players in long-sleeve shirts – a far cry from the sexy singlets and shorts that had been announced.

In a comment published in 2015 on a US website which had picked up the *New York Times* article and relayed it as is, England player Gillian Sayell was categoric. *"I played in Mexico 71 and can put the record straight that we did NOT play in hot pants and pink and white goal posts! As for beauty parlors, I've never read such utter nonsense. Not sure where you got this information but it is totally misinformed"*. While the overt sexualization of the players at the tournament would appear to be an urban myth, therefore, De Haro was not exaggerating when he said that the focus was on the feminine aspect of the event. Those working at the tournament, particular the ones providing the half-time entertainment, wore entirely prink dresses, while more surprisingly still, the crossbars and goalposts were painted with pink and white stripes. Clichés that were rife at the time also got an airing according Mexican player Lourdes de la Rosa: " *Sometimes at training sessions people would shout 'Go home and do the cooking! Go and do the washing-up!' at us."*

Despite these sexist comments, the players provided a quality product out on the pitch. Group A which featured Mexico, Argentina and England saw 13 goals across the three matches played in the capital. After their opening victory against Argentina, the host country thrashed England 4-0, with that defeat for the English coming just a few days after a 4-1 reverse at the hand of the *Albiceleste,* for whom Elba Selva bagged all four goals. *"Our match against Argentina was incredibly tough,"* said Caleb. *"Two of our players ended up in plaster casts..."* And while Selva emerged physically unscathed, little did she realize that an unexpected turn of events was just a few days away, and that she had already played her last match of the tournament...

After the group stage, Mexico and Argentina were first and second in group A which sent them through to the semi-finals, while England were at the bottom of the pile and destined for play-off to determine their final standing.

In Group B, it was between France, Denmark and Italy to see who would go through to the semi-finals. The matches were played in the city of Guadalajara, located over 500 kilometers away from the Mexico City. Denmark got their campaign under way by cruising to a 3-0 win over the French.

*"It was a good match,"* said Augustesen, who scored one of her country's goals. *"I remember that France played pretty well."* Nevertheless, the French were not good enough to see off Italy in the second group match, on 21 August, where they slipped to a 1-0 loss. The Danes and Italians then played out a draw, with both of them already through to the next stage of the competition, while *les Bleues* were consigned to a match for fifth place against England after finishing bottom of the group.

With a week between the end of the group stage and the semi-finals, the Danish team take advantage of the break to do some sight-seeing. *"We visited a number of places including the pyramids and the floating gardens of Xochimilco. We also spent some time relaxing in the pool,"* said one-time Lazio striker Augustesen, who became a lot less relaxed, however, when the team bus broke down right in the middle of the Guadalajara desert. *"There were no toilets or air conditioning in our old bus. We had to pee out in the desert in the middle of these enormous cactuses. It was a wonderful view, mind you – like a picture postcard..."* After a wait of several hours and a telephone call from the nearest village they could find, the Italian team bus finally came to their aid, and they emerged unscathed but with a few stories to tell...

Not everyone was that lucky, however. During a trip from the hotel to the training camp, Argentinian team bus hit a van. Eight players were injured but fortunately there were no broken bones. "*All I know is that our top scorer Elba Selva won't be playing on Saturday (in the semi-final against Denmark) as she's hurt both her legs,*" Betty Garcia, one of the players involved in the accident, said to the local press at the time, adding that at least three players would be out for that match. Things were taking a turn for the worse for the *Albiceleste,* whose pre-tournament had already been hampered by various obstacles.

"*When we set off for Mexico, we had no cleats, no medical staff, no physios, no coach and jerseys that fell apart the first time you washed them,*" said Betty Garcia when talking to *Pagina 12,* and Selva spoke of similar conditions in an interview with another website, *La Nación.* "*The hosts covered the hotel, the food, the medical costs and the clothes. They gave us cleats. I remember that we had to walk around in them before the matches to break them in. We felt like we were playing in high heels!*" Some players had travelled out there without any money and took to selling signed photos of the team to earn a few pesos so that they could write home to friends and family.

After slipping to a defeat in their opener against Mexico, the *Albiceleste* ended up getting a helping hand from an unexpected source. Norberto Rozas, a former footballer from Argentina who moved into coaching, offered to manage the team for the rest of the tournament after watching their first match. Nevertheless, and given the circumstances, it was going to take more than the arrival of a makeshift coach and a few pairs of new cleats to defeat the reigning *"world champions"* from Denmark.

Having arrived in Mexico with a squad of 17, Argentina came into their semi-final against Denmark on 28 August with three players out injured and another five struggling for form after the coach accident, and they indeed took a hiding, crashing out 5-0 in the Azteca Stadium in Mexico City. The following day, *la Verde* met Italy in the second semi-final. As mentioned in the previous chapter, a bunch of supporters prevented the Italian players from getting to sleep by making a racket outside their hotel all night, and worse still, the referee went on to disallow two perfectly valid goals for the *Azzurre* during the match! Despite all of these extremely unfavorable conditions for their opponents, the Mexicans barely scraped home 2-1, but that was enough to see them into the final to face Denmark.

Knowing full well that the matches at the *Mundial* were bringing in thousands of spectators, the Mexican team had legitimate expectations of some form of financial compensation, so they asked for a million pesos (around $320,000) to share among the squad of 16 plus the coach, the fitness trainer and the doctor. This provoked a stand-off with the tournament organizing committee and its president, Jaime de Haro. The local press accused the players of demanding money even though they were only amateurs. *"Of course we were amateurs,"* said Alicia Vargas, the first women's footballer to be elected to the Mexican Hall of Fame in 2018, *"but we were the ones playing. If they didn't want to pay us, they should have made the tickets for the matches free."* The threats by the Mexicans that they would not play the final had little effect, with De Haro ready to put together another Mexico team or one made up of players from other participating nations rather than cancel the final. *"In the end, we decided to play the match for the spectators' sake, as it wasn't their fault that this situation had come about,"* Vargas concluded. In an interview with the *BBC* website, a number of England players confirmed that they had not received so much as a penny for their part in the *Mundial*...

England's woes at the tournament were not confined to the financial hardship of the players. In the play-off for fifth place, they went down 3-2 to France courtesy of goals from Armelle Binard, Jocelyne Henry and Ghislaine Royer. In the other play-off, Argentina and Italy battled it out for a place on the podium, and the journey from Mexico City to Guadalajara turned out to be another harrowing experience for the team from South America... *"We were worried we wouldn't make it,"* recalled Marta Soler, who was 17 at the time. *"There was so much turbulence that if we'd* have been allowed to open the windows, I think a few players would've jumped out..." The trip was a bridge too far for the *Albiceleste* who went down 4-0 to the *Squadra Azzurra*, for whom Elisabetta Vignotto bagged three goals.

The third-place play-off attracted an attendance of 50,000, but that was nothing compared with the crowd that flocked to see Denmark take on the Mexicans in the final on 5 September. Having heard what had happened to the Italians on the night before their semi-final against the hosts, the team decided to call the Danish embassy in Mexico, who found a dozen or so families from Denmark living nearby who were willing to put them up for the night. The sole purpose of this maneuver of course was to get a good night's sleep before the most important match of their lives!

*"I remember there being so many people in the stadium,"* said Augustesen. *"Personally I tried to block them out and focus on my game."* But when there are 110,000 of them, as was the case for the final that day in the Azteca Stadium, that is easier said than done. The attendance is certainly worth closer analysis.

On 17 March 2019, a large number of articles in the press carried the information that the record attendance for a women's club fixture had been beaten when no fewer than 60,739 spectators flocked to the Metropolitano Stadium in Madrid to see Atletico Madrid take on Barcelona. In France, the highest attendance for a top-flight women's league match came on 13 April 2019, when 26,000 fans attended the clash between Lyon and Paris Saint-Germain at the Groupama Stadium. For international matches, the outright record goes back to the (official) Women's World Cup final between USA and China on 10 July 1999, a title showdown which attracted 90,185 spectators. Organizers of the recent FIFA Women's World Cup in France in 2019 could only dream of matching the record of the Mexico – Denmark final on 5 September 1971, which is probably the best attended women's soccer match of all time, giving this *Mundial "a special place in history"* according to Augustesen.

There was also a special place in history for the Danish attacker. Just a month after her parents had been reluctant to send her over to Mexico, Augustesen notched a hat-trick in front of 110,000 spectators. Despite being right-footed, she scored all three with her left, the first of which was due to a terrible handling error by the Mexican goalkeeper Elvira Aracén. *"Augustesen's shot presented no danger,"* a local newspaper said at the time. *"The goalkeeper Aracén dived but when the ball was in her reach, her fingers turned into a bar of soap and the shot passed over the top of them, silencing the crowd..."* This error could be put down to the fact that, unlike the other goalies in the competition, Aracén did not wear gloves during the tournament, as can be seen on the cover of this publication. One explanation for this is that conditions were very dry in Mexico at that time of year, but her choice had no influence on the other two goals. The second in particular was a thing of beauty, much like Pedro Miguel Pauleta's past face Fabien Barthez in the traditional French grudge match between Paris Saint-Germain and Marseille on 25 April 2004 (one that is worth seeking out on YouTube).

Denmark ended up cruising to a 3-0 victory and defending their title of *"world champions"* that they had won the previous year in Italy. *"We were all happy of course and dancing around and hugging each other,"* the young hat-trick hero said, *"and running around the pitch with the trophy."* The silverware had been provided by main sponsors *Martini & Rossi* and depicted an angel sporting a Greek crown with a soccer ball at its feet. It was given the majestic name of *"Winged Goddess"*, and according to the archives of Mexican newspaper *El Universal*, it was made of gold and stood 70 centimeters tall.

The following day there was a medals ceremony in a bullfighting arena. *"I remember the Mexicans giving me some funny looks because I'd scored three goals the day before!"* said Augustesen, who then returned from Mexico to her native Holbæk with *"only a few dollars and a suitcase to get me started in my hometown"*.

Upon their return to Denmark, the team were received like royalty at Copenhagen city hall. Understandably, young Augustesen's exploits had made it across the Atlantic with a number of Italian clubs looking to sign her up. She was keen to finish her schooling, and waited until she was 18 before penning a deal with Bologna. The striker went on to have an incredible career in the country, finishing top-scorer in the women's top flight eight times, notching an incredible 42 goals in the 1977 season. She also won the league title six times and the Italian Cup on three occasions. She went on to ply her trade with Lazio, Cagliari, Lecce and Modena, scoring 600 goals in a career spanning over 20 years in Italy. She was never picked to represent Denmark officially but was nevertheless inducted into her country's Hall of Fame on 20 March 2017, more than 45 years after her historic hat-trick in Mexico. Better late than never...

# RESULTS FROM THE
# *MUNDIAL* 1971

## Group A

15 August 1971: Mexico 3 - 1 Argentina

21 August 1971: Argentina 4 - 1 England

22 August 1971: Mexico 4 - 0 England


## Group B

18 August 1971: Denmark 3 - 0 France

21 August 1971: Italy 1 - 0 France

22 August 1971: Denmark 1 - 1 Italy


## Semi-finals

28 August 1971: Denmark 5 - 0 Argentina

29 August 1971: Mexico 2 - 1 Italy


## Fifth place play-off:

28 August 1971: France 3 - 2 England

## Third place play-off

4 September 1971: Italy 4 - 0 England

## Final

5 September 1971: Denmark 3 - 0 Mexico

Source: *Erik Garin - Rec. Sport Soccer Statistics Foundation*

# THE HISTORY OF THE WORLD WOMEN'S FOOTBALL INVITATIONAL TOURNAMENT

On the other side of the Pacific, in Asia, women were looking to emulate the feats of the early 1970s of their European and Central American counterparts. Women's soccer was even less developed in Asia than it was in Europe, however. Many national associations struggled to get players, and the lack of numbers were the main arguments put forward by Asian men's football committees for not officially recognizing women's soccer. Since they were considered as dissident and rivals to FIFA and its affiliated federations, independent women's soccer associations looking to develop the sport were looked down on, afforded no support from the federations and naturally had no hope of organizing officially recognized tournaments. FIFA and the men's soccer federations therefore had the final say when it came to the survival of independent bodies looking to further the women's game.

This unhealthy form of reliance did not stop certain organizations from seeing the light of day, however. The most noteworthy of these was the Asian Ladies Football Confederation (ALFC) founded in 1968. This particularly body was made up of women from upper social classes, many of them married or related to people in executive roles in men's soccer. Within a few years of is inception, the ALFC already had 11 member associations including Japan, Hong Kong, Taiwan, Australia and India. It was a feminist organization, and very soon was pressing for women to be able to participate in the same competitions as men. As such, they created an inaugural Asian championship, held in Hong Kong in 1975 and which was roughly equivalent to the men's Asian Cup of Nations organized every four years by the Asian Football Confederation (AFC).

This first women's edition, held 19 years after the inaugural men's Asian Cup of Nations – was a resounding success! The matches drew crowds of between 2,000 and 11 000 spectators, and 11,573 attended the final at the Hong Kong Stadium, which was also broadcast live on local television. Buoyed by this promising first attempt, the ALFC decided to organize further Asian championships every two year.

The women heading up the ALFC were ambitious and looking to play the same competitions as the men, and as such decided to contact FIFA on 10 February 1976. They informed the international governing body that a world cup would be held in Hong Kong the following year – a proposition refused by FIFA and its president João Havelange, who declared that they alone were the only ones able to organize that competition. As it so happened, the Republic of China Football Association (ROFCA) agreed to recognize women's soccer in Taiwan at around the same time. This was during the period when the country was divided, with Mao Zedong's People's Republic of China on the one hand and Chiang Kai-shek's Taiwan on the other, and it was the latter via its federation (ROFCA) which had officially recognized women's soccer.

As Xavier Breuil explains in his thesis "*The history of women's soccer in Europe from the Great War to the present day*", FIFA was not able to refuse to allow one of its affiliated federations to host a tournament. With ROFCA having officially recognized women's soccer, it was thus able to realize the dreams of the ALFC to host an international competition. FIFA for its part merely demanded that the tournament not be given the name "*World Cup*", but also requested that European federations not send their national team or indeed clubs, under the pretext that this new ROFCA-organized tournament was a private initiative. And FIFA naturally took the opportunity to remind the various European federations how the other tournaments organized by the Italian businessmen of the FIEFF in the early 1970s had panned out...

The ALFC and ROFCA however were promising to cover all of the costs of those invited, and thus it was that a number of clubs had no hesitation in taking part in the inaugural edition of the World Women's Football Invitational Tournament in Taipei in 1978, despite the governing body's recommendations. These included Stade de Reims (France), HJK Helsinki (Finland) and Sting Soccer Club (USA), who found themselves taking on national teams from Australia and Thailand. Three more tournaments would go on to be held in the Taiwanese capital throughout the 1980s.

Faced with the success of the women's tournaments organized by ROFCA and the ALFC, FIFA was shaken out of its indifference and began to take the women's game seriously, primarily out of fear of losing its grip on women's soccer to independent organizations. The governing body's objective was clear – to demonstrate that it was all-powerful on the world soccer scene. And to do this, it would have to get the women's game back into the fold.

26

# WORLD WOMEN'S FOOTBALL INVITATIONAL TOURNAMENT 1978

**Location**: Taiwan (Republic of China)

**Organized by**: The Republic of China Football Association (ROFCA)

**Date**: 9 October – 23 October 1978

I t took 20 long years for France, under Aimé Jacquet, to win a second soccer World Cup. Two decades before Zinedine Zidane worked his magic at the Stade de France, it was the women of the Stade de Reims club who represented France at the first edition of the World Women's Football Invitational Tournament (WWFIT) held in Taipei in 1978. And those women certainly flew the flag for their country in the best possible way, coming home from Taipei with the title of world champions. Pierre Geoffroy's charges admittedly had to share that honor with Finland, but that fact should take nothing away from their admirable performance which was one of the finest in the history of women's soccer in France, and yet probably the least well-known. At that time, over half of the France team was made up of players from Reims. Their excellent results on the pitch coupled with the considerable influence of their coach, journalist Pierre Geoffroy, meant that Stade de Reims were regularly invited by national associations to take part in tournaments designed to promote women's soccer. The Reims players used to call these games *'propaganda matches'*. "*We'd say back then that we were going off on tour,*" said Isabelle Musset in a report by Yvonne Debeaumarché entitled *'Les filles du stade'*.

Having been invited by ROFCA, who were covering all of their costs, the Stade de Reims team took off from Orly airport on 6 August 1978, arriving on the island of Taiwan some three days later, the journey being abnormally long due to a 48-hour stopover in Bahrain! Under military escort – as was the case throughout the tournament – the women from the Champagne region of France finally got to settle into their comfortable downtown hotel in Taipei. However, on 9 October –the day that the event was due to start – a typhoon hit the Taiwan capital, literally flooding the stadia and forcing the organizers to push back the start of the tournament by 48 hours. As a result, certain matches that were meant to be played during the evening were moved up to the daytime, which meant a drop in attendance and therefore profits for the organizers.

The main thing however was that the tournament actually took place, and it did so in two phases. The 13 teams were divided into three groups, with the top two of each qualifying for the final phase, which itself took the form of a mini-championship. The team finishing in first place at the end of the latter group stage would then be crowned world champions.

**Reims squad**: *Butzig, Vatin, Brassart, Bassier, Dormois, Delahaye, Thomas, Moine, Roy, Pigeon, Vilarinho, Musset, Binard, Batteux, Scharo, Abar, Souef, Plantegenet*

Geoffroy's squad found themselves in Group C along with Thailand, Helsinki (Finland), Vancouver (Canada) and Northwood

(UK), and they got their campaign off to a flying start, thrashing Thailand 6-0 on 14 October! Renée Delahaye, who was captain of the Reims team, recalled the atmosphere at the match as much as the result. *"It made a real impression! The stadium was full and the atmosphere was extraordinary. There must have been between 5,000 and 25,000 spectators at every match of the tournament. The whole thing was very well organized."* From a sporting perspective, things were not quite so simple for the three-time defending French champions however.

*"The weather was absolutely horrendous and made it tough for us to play our natural game as we were a pretty skilled outfit,"* Delahaye explained. *"They brought soldiers in to mop the pitches, and they used buckets to empty the water out of the stadium! The rain was torrential, the city must have been under almost two feet of water! The typhoon resulted in a flood."* Once the tournament started, the matches were played on paddy fields rather than pitches...

With the tournament starting 48 hours late, the timetable had to be tightened up, and the Reims team ended up playing two matches on 16 October. The first was at 1 pm and saw a win over Northwood 4-1, then at 7 pm they defeated Vancouver, this time 4-0. The French representatives finished their group stage

the following day, 17 October, with at 0-0 draw with Helsinki. *"Some teams like Helsinki and Sting SC who were representing the USA were very gifted technically,"* Delahaye went on. *"They already had a certain amount of experience at the top level. Watching Sting SC play in 1978, we thought that if soccer were to develop in the USA, then the US women would become be very strong."* How right she was!

At the end of the first stage, Stade de Reims were top of Group C, level on points with Finland, and that was also the result after the second stage when the two again could not be separated, although the Reims local newspaper *L'Union* said that the French team could have finished top and been considered the outright winners.

*At the end of the overall standings, Reims were deal level with Helsinki [...] only goal average in the qualifying matches – 14-1 for Stade de Reims, 13-0 for Helsinki – could have swung the balance in favor of the French as they had the better attack. But after so many inconveniences throughout the world tournament, the organizers preferred to declare that there were two equal winners, and both teams linked arms for a lap of honor.*

This arrangement may have been the fairest way of settling things, but it had not been anticipated, and the organizers hastily had to get a new cup and around 20 more medals to cover all of the players in both teams!

*"As far as we were concerned, we were world champions,"* said Delahaye, who knew that she and her team-mates should have taken that lap of honor on their own with just the one trophy in their hands at the closing ceremony on 23 October 1978. They did, however, end up bringing plenty of silverware home with them. Along with the 'World Cup' of course, they picked up four individual awards, for the best goalkeeper (Marie-Louise Butzig), best defender (Delahaye), best midfielder (Véronique Roy) and best attacker (Christine Scharo). A clean sweep!

Centre-forward (and French international) Scharo finished the tournament as top scorer with seven goals. 'General Scharo' as she was known drew comparisons with Mario Kempes. who shot his country to victory on home soil in the 1978 men's world cup in Argentina.

The Stade de Reims players finally got to leave Asia, with memories and awards aplenty, on 26 October, having accomplished their mission.

More than four decades later, looking back at the typhoon, the matches, the full stadia, the presentation of the trophies and the lap of honor – did Stade de Reims record the greatest achievement in the history of French women's soccer back in October 1978? Delahaye is well aware that comparisons across generations are not always reliable, and is more reticent about her group's exploit, despite the fact that no full France women's soccer team has repeated the feat since. *"You can't really compare it with modern soccer. We didn't train as often back then, we didn't earn any money. Soccer was just a hobby for us. You need to look at our performances in relative terms and keep your feet on the ground. Yes, we were world champions, but that's no reason to get carried away with what we did."*

*"We did things we'll remember for as long as we live,"* said the former international, who along with her team-mates acquired unique experiences both on and off the pitch. *"Soccer also gave us friendships that we still have to this day, as the former Stade de Reims players still meet up with one another. Stories like these create life-long ties."* 40 years on, the bonds are stronger than ever.

# RESULTS FROM WORLD WOMEN'S FOOTBALL INVITATIONAL TOURNAMENT 1978

## Group A

11 October 1978: Republic of China 2 - 0 Polynesia

14 October 1978: Copenhagen 0 - 0 SV Seebach (Zurich, Switzerland)

15 October 1978: Republic of China 2 - 0 SV Seebach

16 October 1978: Copenhagen 1 - 0 Polynesia

17 October 1978: SC Seebach 8 - 2 Polynesia

17 October 1978: Republic of China 1 - 0 Copenhagen

## Group B

14 October 1978: Hackås IF (Sweden) 1 - 1 Sting SC

14 October 1978: Australia 1 - 0 Union SC Landhaus (Austria)

15 October 1978: Australia 1 - 1 Sting SC (USA)

15 October 1978: Hackås IF 1 - 0 Union SC Landhaus

16 October 1978: Sting SC 1 - 0 Union SC Landhaus

16 October 1978: Hackås IF 1 - 0 Australia

## Group C

11 October 1978: Thailand 4 - 0 Northwood (England)

14 October 1978: HJK Helsinki 4 - 0 Vancouver

14 October 1978: Stade de Reims 6 - 0 Thailand

15 October 1978: Vancouver 3 - 0 Northwood

15 October 1978: HJK Helsinki 3 - 0 Thailand

16 October 1978: Stade de Reims 4 - 1 Northwood

16 October 1978: Stade de Reims 4 - 0 Vancouver

16 October 1978: HJK Helsinki 6 - 0 Vancouver

17 October 1978: Stade de Reims 0 - 0 HJK Helsinki

17 October 1978: Thailand 0 - 0 Vancouver

**Play-offs for the top six places**

18 October 1978: Republic of China 4 - 1 Hackås IF

18 October 1978: HJK Helsinki 2 - 0 Sting SC

18 October 1978: Stade de Reims 1 - 0 SV Seebach

19 October 1978: Stade de Reims 5 - 0 Hackås IF

19 October 1978: Republic of China 0 - 2 Sting SC

19 October 1978: HJK Helsinki 0-0 SV Seebach

20 October 1978: Stade de Reims 0 - 0 Sting SC

20 October 1978: Hackås IF 1 - 1 SV Seebach

20 October 1978: Republic of China 0 - 0 HJK Helsinki

21 October 1978: HJK Helsinki 4 - 0 Hackås IF

21 October 1978: Republic of China 0 - 0 Stade de Reims

21 October 1978: Sting SC 3 - 2 SV Seebach

**Final standings**

1. HJK Helsinki and Stade de Reims
2. Republic of China
3. Sting SC
4. SV Seebach
5. Hackås IF
6. Copenhagen
7. Australia
8. Thailand
9. Northwood
10. Union SC Landhaus
11. Polynesia
12. Vancouver

# THE HISTORY OF
# THE *MUNDIALITO*

A s the 1980s rolled around, UEFA and FIFA were beginning to take more of an interest in women's soccer, but a number of independent organizations such as the ALFC were still doing their utmost to promote the sport. In a letter addressed to FIFA dated 1 April 1981, the ALFC declared that it *"felt that the time had come for the women's soccer associations and their clubs to federate into a body that would defend its rights (...) and promote the sport more effectively around the world"*. While they waited for the international soccer federation to heed their call, the ALFC and its affiliated associations organized a new international tournament in Japan in 1981 alongside those being held in Taiwan.

The new event was called *Mundialito* and was directly inspired by a men's competition of the same name held a few months earlier. It was played out in relative obscurity in Montevideo, Uruguay from 30 December 1980 to 10 January 1981, and featured the six teams to have already won the World Cup since it was held for the first time in 1930. Uruguay, West Germany, Brazil, Italy, Argentina and England were thus invited to this tournament that was organized to mark the 50th anniversary of the first men's World Cup played in Uruguay. England were the only team to turn down the opportunity and were replaced by the Netherlands, who had been finalists in1974 and 1978. The *Mundialito* in Uruguay went under the radar as far as the general public were concerned but featured some of the great names of the beautiful game, including Diego Maradona, Mario Kempes, Sócrates, Franco Baresi, Carlo Ancelotti and Karl-Heinz Rummenigge. Uruguay ended up being crowned 'champion of champions' after a 2-1 win over Brazil.

The first women's *Mundialito* was held in Japan from 6–9 September 1981 during the Portopia' 81 international exposition held to inaugurate an artificial island called Port Island in Kobe built between 1966 and 1981. The tournament featured four teams – Japan, Italy, England and Denmark – with everyone playing one another in a round robin and the team finishing first in the group winning the tournament. Buoyed by a 9-0 win over the host country, Italy finished atop the group on goal difference, winning the inaugural *Mundialito*.

Four more editions were held between 1984 and 1988 and were organized by the Italian soccer federation. The *Squadra Azzurra* won three of the five overall (1981, 1984 and 1986), closely followed by England who won in 1985 and 1988. Carolina Morace, who was capped 153 times by Italy, is the only player to score at least one goal at each of the five tournaments. This series of 'mini World Cups' also drove the US soccer federation to finally create a women's section. After the incredible performances of Sting SC from Texas in China in 1984 – which will be detailed later in this book – the US Soccer Federation (USSF) was convinced that the time had come to create its own national team. Their resolve was further strengthened when they received an invitation to take part in the third edition of the *Mundialito* in 1985. From 22 July – 4 August that year, the USSF called up 70 players to Baton Rouge in Louisiana during the National Sports Festival, which was the largest amateur multisport event in the country at the time. 17 players were ultimately selected to got to Italy to play in the tournament which started a few days later, and thus it was that the USA played their first official match against Italy on 18 August 1985 in Jesolo.

An article published on *FIFA.com* on 4 March 2010 provides come interesting background on the Algarve Cup, a women's tournament featuring the top countries in the world every year. *"The competition attracts so many good teams that it is also known as the Mundialito or mini-World Cup."* It does not take a leap of faith to imagine that the Italian *Mundialitos* of the 1980s were the inspiration behind the name chosen by the Portuguese Soccer Federation when it created its event in 1994 ...

# MUNDIALITO 1984

**Location**: Italy

**Organized by**: The Italian Soccer Federation

**Date**: 19 August – 26 August 1984

I taly ended up having to wait for another 14 years before hosting another Women's World Cup on home soil. After the resounding success of the *Coppa del Mondo* won by the *Squadra Azzurra* in 1970, the Italian soccer federation came back 14 years later with another (rather minimalist) tournament held from 19–26 August 1984, featuring four teams as opposed to the eight of 1970. The name was also changed from *Coppa del Mondo* to *Mundialito*. The suffix "-ito" is often used in Spanish as a diminutive for a person or an object, making the *Mundialito* a *"mini-World Cup"*. The tournament was also not held around the entire country but in two towns near Venice just over 10 miles apart, Caorle and Jesolo. Both were tourist hot-spots ready to welcome locals and foreigners alike to their venues, namely the Giovanni Chiggiato stadium with a capacity of 2,500, and the Armando Picchi stadium which could house around 5,000 at the time. The format was the same as in the first two *Coppa del Mondo* tournaments held in Italy and Mexico in 1970 and 1971. The teams first played a group phase before facing off either for third place or for the title. The four countries who took part in the *Mundialito* 84 – the second of its kind after the one organized in Japan in 1981 – were host nation Italy, England, West Germany and Belgium. Of all the various *Mundialitos* held during the 1980s, this one in 1984 was the only one to have solely European countries involved, with the Belgian press even referring to it as a European championship rather than a World Cup. The players from that country were of a similar opinion, with goalkeeper Anne Noë saying *"It wasn't much of a World Cup, we saw it more as a small-scale European championship"*. Based on the line-up, it was difficult to say otherwise...

The Italian press on the other hand were more than willing to cover the event and refer to it as a genuine World Cup. The country's main sporting dailies, namely the *Gazzetta dello Sport* and the *Corriere dello Sport* devoted a number of articles to the tournament, and even more general newspapers such as *La Repubblica* – which has one of the widest circulations in the country – featured the competition. *"It generated a lot of interest at the time,"* recalled Feriana Ferraguzzi, who played for Italy in the *Mundialito* in 1984. *"We even had press conferences before and after the matches."* Even more impressive was the fact that some of the games were shown on public access television on the *Rai 3* channel. Rai is the biggest Italian audiovisual group and judged the event to be worth covering. Italy after all were the defending champions, having won the inaugural edition in Japan in 1981. England had made it to the final of the first official European championships organized by UEFA just three months earlier, losing to Sweden. West Germany meanwhile had a very competitive squad even back then, not to mention a historical rivalry with the *Squadra Azzurra*. *"We hated them!"* said Fery Ferraguzzi, in reference to the bad blood that had built up through the legendary matches between the two teams at the men's World Cups in Mexico in 1970 and Spain in 1982. The 1970 semi-final ended up with Italy winning 4-3 over West Germany in what came to be known as the *"Partita del Secolo"* (*"the match of the century"*) in Italian footballing circles. Belgium appeared to be the outsiders, but it would turn out that coach Albert Bers' charges had not made the trip down south purely to make up the numbers.

The tournament kicked off on 19 August 1984, a few hours after the opening ceremony and presentation of the teams in a packed

Giovanni Chiggiato stadium. All four nations were obviously looking to finish in the top two of the one and only group and thus qualify for the final, while those finishing third and fourth would play off for third place. The opening match of the *Mundialito 84* was the ideal curtain-raiser, pitting Italy against West Germany, but this dream fixture turned into a nightmare for the *Azzurre* who slipped to a 2-1 defeat. The following day, 20 August, Belgium and European Championship runners-up England played out a 1-1 draw. With tournament being packed into a very tight schedule running for just one week, every team had to play their four matches within the space of seven days. Given those conditions, and even taking into account that the games were only 80 minutes long, recovery become a key factor. And so when Belgium had to play Italy on 21 August after the host country had had an extra day's rest, the match soon became one-way traffic with Ettore Recagni's women cantering to a 4-0 win. *"And believe it or not, the Gazzetta dello Sport wrote in their article that I'd had a very good match!"* said Standard Liege keeper Noë, seeing the funny side of things as she pored over her archives. *"We had a really short tactical discussion before the matches, but there was no video at the time. The main thing we did back then was try to rest between matches."* The Italians on the other hand had opted for a different strategy between games. *"The weather was incredibly hot throughout the week but it actually wasn't that tough physically,"* explained Ferraguzzi. *"We went to spa baths to recover between matches, and there was also backroom staff who gave us massages, as well as a fitness coach who swore by cryotherapy. It was the first time that we'd used cold baths for recovery. Well to be honest, we'd never actually heard of cryotherapy before that."* It was the kind of preparation that befitted a professional outfit, and it would go on to play a crucial role throughout the tournament.

At the end of the round-robin stage, West Germany finished first in the group after wins over Italy (2-1) and England (2-0) and a defeat to Belgium (0-2). The Italians ran out second after drawing with England, who failed to win any of their three group games and who were certainly a step behind the Italians when it came to diet and optimizing their recovery time. "*We often used to have seemingly never-ending dinners after international matches with the opposition,*" Ferraguzzi recalled. "*We Italians were a pretty genteel crowd, but the English... they certainly let themselves go when it came to the alcohol. I remember one or two of them ending up on the floor, blind drunk. Probably due to the heat (laughs)!*"

Despite that, the Three Lionesses still managed to overcome Belgium 2-1 in the match for third place that was played on 25 August 1984 in Caorle, "*a defeat that was not deserved*" according to Belgian newspaper *Het Laatste Nieuws* after the game. Despite the fact that this loss consigned them to fourth and last place, coach Bers preferred to accentuate the positives, saying: "*we played a good tournament with a decent fourth-placed finish and first and foremost good performances against Germany and England in the group stage*".

The day after the match for third place, the host country once again faced off against their bitter rivals from Germany in the hope of taking revenge for their opening-match loss. The match was shown live on *Rai 3*, with Italian journalists Giorgio Martino and Gianfranco de Laurentiis providing the commentary. The local media were not very optimistic ahead of the final, as illustrated by an article which was published on 26 August – the day of the match – in *La Repubblica*: "*Italy are not favorites against a Germany team that is stronger and more experienced.*" The author must have regretted penning those lines half-an-hour into the match, by which time the *Squadra Azzurra* were already three goals to the good against a Germany team that seemed completely out of its depth. Carolina Morace (8'), Rose Reilly (20') and Elisabetta Vignotto (30', penalty) took the favorites apart in the space of just 30 minutes.

With 5,000 spectators behind them who had come to cheer them on at the Armando Picchi stadium in Jesolo, the Italians nursed their three-goal advantage through to half time, and despite the tempo slowing down in the second half and West Germany pegging one back barely five minutes after the break, Italy were never really in any danger throughout the final, and ran out convincing 3-1 winners. The three goal scorers – Morace, Vignotto and Reilly – would all go on to be inducted into various Halls of Fame at different times. Morace, who was top-scorer at the *Mundialito* 84 with four goals, became the first woman to be voted in among the legends of Italian soccer in 2014. Three years later, she was joined by team-mate Vignotto, while Reilly's career took a different path. Her aim from the outset was to be a professional player, and she left her native Scotland to play simultaneously in France, for Stade de Reims, and Italy. *"I played with my Italian club Lecce on the Saturday afternoon then I'd fly to Paris on Sunday to play with Stade de Reims,"* center-forward Reilly explained. She was banned by the Scottish soccer federation for going to play abroad, but was taken on by the *Squadra Azzurra*. Despite having won 10 caps for Scotland in the early 1970s. And in 2007, Reilly became the first woman to be inducted into the prestigious Scottish Hall of Fame.

Getting back to the final of the *Mundialito* 1984, the entire match is available to be watched on YouTube. I made an effort to study the whole game to ensure that the (male) referee, Sante Zaza of Italy, had been as impartial as possible. and in my opinion he was. Should you choose to watch it, you will also see both goalkeepers picking up back-passes from team-mates, ball-girls dressed from head to toe in pink placing the ball in the arc ahead of corners, and photographers wandering onto the pitch to capture the celebrations of the home players after each goal. And if you look very closely, you will see a French flag attached to a stadium barrier – who knows, perhaps a Reims supporter had come to cheer on Rose Reilly...

After the trophy was presented out on the pitch followed by some after-match interviews, the now two-time defending champions were able to go and interact with their supporters. *"It was one of the first times that we got to sign autographs after a match,"* recalled

Ferraguzzi, who would end up winning 99 caps for Italy. Usually a play-maker for the *Azzurre,* she operated as a sweeper in the final of the *Mundialito* 84, a tournament which she viewed as a great success: "*It meant that the general public had a greater awareness of us as we got a lot of coverage in the press. The journalists were all surprised to see that women could also be good at soccer. It was good advertising for our sport.*"

Recagni's squad would continue this good promotional work less than two months after their title-win in Jesolo, with a new challenge awaiting them in one of FIFA's preferred launching pads for women's soccer – China.

# THE HISTORY OF THE TOURNAMENTS IN THE REPUBLIC OF CHINA

**W**ith its virtual 'Asian Cup of Nations' and World Women's Football Invitational Tournament (WWFIT) co-organized with ROFCA between the 1970s and 1980s, the ALFC proved to FIFA that women's soccer was capable of generating and exciting crowds (not to mention profits). The idea of organizing a fully-fledged Women's World Cup began to take root in the minds of executives at the sport's governing body. It was also more than probable that they were fearful of losing a potential goose laying golden eggs to independent bodies like the ALFC. A book entitled '*FIFA 1904 – 2004: a century of football*' which was described as being the "*first and indeed only official work by FIFA on the history and impact of football in society,*" features the following passage:

> *Faced with pressure from the ALFC to create an international organization at the beginning of the 1980s, FIFA finally began to take women's football seriously and even looked to aid its development. The executive committee suggested that FIFA organize an international tournament, even if only to show that it controlled all of the sport.*

FIFA was not the only body that was sitting up and taking notice of the ALFC and ROFCA. As mentioned in the chapter about the WWFITs, China was divided in two in the 1980s, with the People's Republic of China on the mainland, with Beijing as the capital, and the island Republic of China, also known as Taiwan. Both countries wanted to be recognized as the only official China in the eyes of the world and of the main global sporting bodies, including of course FIFA. The Republic of China had far less diplomatic clout than its continental rival, which led for example to the county having to change the name of its federation in 1981. No more could it be referred to as ROFCA (Republic of China Football Association), but rather CTFA (Chinese Taipei Football Association).

Despite this enforced change of designation, the freshly minted CTFA continued to organize its various women's soccer competitions – a field in which nationalist China was some way ahead of its communist rival. World Women's Football Invitational Tournaments were held every three years, and in 1981, 1984 and 1987, they once again attracted the major global nations, as was the case when Stade de Reims won the event in 1978. Since the CTFA was affiliated to FIFA, the latter could not refuse to allow them to hold these tri-annual tournaments. Furthermore, in 1981 they validated competition rules and circulated them among the various affiliated federations. And from that point onwards, national soccer associations around the world did not hesitate to send their best representatives to Taiwan for the highly anticipated WWFITs, particularly since the accommodation costs and half of the travel budget of teams that were invited were covered by the CTFA, which itself received financial support from the ALFC. As such, there was no reason for any teams not to attend…

This fledgling recognition did not go unnoticed by the People's Republic of China, and in an attempt to make up lost ground on its neighbor, it looked to start developing women's soccer. Its first women's professional team featuring 12 players was created in the city of Xi'an in the summer of 1979, less than a year after the inaugural edition of the WWFIT in Taipei. It was followed three years later by the first women's team in Beijing. Also in 1982, the Chinese minister for sport organized the first national women's soccer championship with 10 teams taking part. Over the next two years that it was held, the number of participating teams went up to 27 in 1983 and 35 in 1984.

The People's Republic of China rapidly followed in its rival's footsteps in organizing international tournaments. It held its inaugural continental competition in 1983, called the Guangzhou Women's Tournament. The city of Guangzhou, formerly known as Canton, hosted two national teams from abroad for a women's soccer tournament for the first time, namely Japan and Singapore, with the entry field completed by six other Chinese teams. On 15 December 1983, just a month after the tournament in Guangzhou, the Chinese national women's soccer team was officially created. Again on the initiative of the ministry of sports and with the support of the Chinese soccer federation, continental China organized the Xi'an Women's Tournament in October 1984, with the blessing of FIFA and featuring Japan, Italy, Australia, USA (represented by the Sting Soccer Club) and four Chinese provincial teams.

In response to this second tournament organized by the People's Republic of China, the CTFA hosted the third edition of the WWFIT two months later, in December 1984. Women's soccer thus found itself caught up in a geopolitical conflict, but at least it was putting the sport in the spotlight. The main long-term aim of the two Chinas was clear – to get one over on their rival by hosting the first 'trial-run' of the FIFA Women's World Cup that was becoming more and more likely as time went on...

XIAN
INTERNATIONAL
WOMEN'S FOOTBALL
INVITATIONAL
TOURNAMENT
1984

10.14-10.26

PROGRAM

1984年西安国际女子足球邀请赛

秩序册

# XI'AN WOMEN'S TOURNAMENT

**Location**: China

**Organized by**: The Chinese Soccer Federation

**Date**: 14 October – 26 October 1984

Whenever people talk of the pioneers of women's soccer in France, conversation soon turns to Stade de Reims. Established 1968 primarily by Pierre Geoffroy, the women's team rapidly rose to become the standard-bearer for French women's soccer on the global stage. On the other side of the Atlantic, a US equivalent first saw the light of day at the start of the 1970s.

Looking for common threads in the development of Reims and Dallas is no easy task, despite the fact that those two cities can be seen as the birthplace of women's soccer in their respective countries. In 1973, 12 years before the national team's first official match at the *Mundialito,* the first ever women's soccer team in the USA was established in Dallas. It was called the Sting Soccer Club, in reference to the film of the same name featuring Paul Newman and Robert Redford that was released that year. Sting SC was made up solely of under-19 players under the auspices of new coach Bill Kinder, who 11 years later would take that very team to the end of the Silk Road in China, to Xi'an in the province of Shaanxi.

*"The model of The Sting Soccer Club focused on discipline, hard work, skill development, and fitness training that was truly uncommon at the time,"* the official website says in the section dealing with origins of the team. *"It is certain that the unique model of respect, discipline, hard work, and team unity contributed to the immense success that would follow."*

The almost military discipline would indeed go on to bear fruit, as of the first nine national under-19 soccer championships, Kinder's teams would win five of them, with an incredible record of 400 wins and just nine defeats! In the 1981-1982 season, Sting SC did not lose a single match, recording 47 wins. Its incredible domination of the domestic scene meant that the Texan club was soon receiving invitations from national associations to play in events all around the world – again like Stade de Reims.

In 1976, the Sting Soccer Club travelled to Mexico to play a curtain-raiser for a men's first division match, with the US youngsters taking on a local side in front of 35,000 spectators! This was the first time in the history of US women's soccer that a team had been invited to play abroad. Two years later, in 1978, the Texans were asked to participate in the inaugural World Women's Football Invitational Tournament in Taipei, where they would finish third behind joint winners Reims and Helsinki and the team from Taipei. This remarkable performance saw ROFCA and the ALFC invite them back three years later in 1981, when Sting SC finished ninth out of 14 teams in the second edition of the WWFIT. At the time, the Taiwanese organizers had had a rather strange idea of asking the various teams taking part in the tournament to prepare a show for the end of the tournament, as Sylvie Béliveau, who was co-coach of the Canadian team at the WWFIT 1987 confirms: *"We had to create a dance for the end of the competition. A banquet had been organized and each of the teams had to perform on stage... Some of the shows were pretty decent, but when you've only had a day or two's rest between matches and you know the standards required of you in terms of on-pitch performances, spending your evenings rehearsing a show is the last thing you want to be doing."*

Thanks to their performances on the domestic and international stages, Sting SC were increasingly in demand. When the 1984 Summer Olympics in Los Angeles came around, the All-China Sports Federation (a Chinese sporting non-governmental organization) contacted the US soccer federation, asking then president Werner Fricker if an American team could be sent to China to take part in the Xi'an international women's tournament organized by the Chinese Federation under the auspices of FIFA. Unfortunately, the Los Angeles Olympics were being held in August and the Chinese tournament was planned for October of the same year. The US Soccer Federation did not have the time to hold trials and set up a national team in the space of two months, and in desperation they turned to Dallas, Texas, where a girls' club had already proved its worth on the international scene and appeared to be the best option to represent the country over in China.

The Chairman of the US Soccer Federation Don Greer contacted Kinder in late August 1984, asking him whether Sting SC could head over to Xi'an for three weeks to represent the USA. Since all of the players were minors, Kinder invited them and their parents to a meeting to outline the project. The Texas Education Agency was also consulted and authorized the players to miss three weeks of school to go to China. Once the formalities had been settled, the Chinese soccer federation faxed all the details over to their US counterparts. For their journey to a communist country, Kinder and his team needed passports, visas and airline tickets to Hong Kong. Once they had landed, they were to take a train to Guangzhou, where they would finally be welcomed by the Chinese soccer federation. Quite the itinerary...

The US delegation which arrived at Dallas-Fort Worth international airport on 12 October 1984 was made up of 40 people, with two coaches and 18 players, some of the latter accompanied by parents or siblings of whom there were 20. Kinder himself paid the airline tickets and was reimbursed later by the families of the players. This added up to no less than $85,000 which was not covered by the US soccer federation, who were not financing the Sting Soccer Club's trip to China. Apparel manufacturers adidas nevertheless designed a kit especially for the players. Rather than their usual club colors of blue and white, they added red to their jersey for the tournament at which they were representing the USA.

A 19-hour flight between Dallas and Hong Kong was merely the beginning of a seemingly never-ending journey to Xi'an. The 40-strong US delegation then began the Chinese leg of their trip with two hours on a train to get to Guangzhou, not knowing what or who would be waiting for them once they got there.

*"Once we arrived in Guangzhou, we waited another two hours for a bus to come,"* Kinder recalled. *"We had no idea who would be coming to meet us. We had quite simply landed in communist China and the Chinese Federation said that they would be looking after us. We arrived and waited in an unknown country, very out of place with our brightly colored clothing, a lot of luggage with us and soccer balls."*

Alicia Tannery Donelan, an 18-year-old Sting SC player at the time, also has vivid memories of the long wait on the platform at Guangzhou station, saying: *"It was pretty warm, the kind of heat that we would have had in Dallas in October"*. After a two-hour wait in weather conditions that they were fortunately accustomed to, the team finally saw the bus hove into view, and they got to meet Kung Hao Chun, their guide and interpreter for the entirety of their trip. Another 45-minute journey then followed across the Chinese countryside as they headed to another airport. *"It was beautiful country. We passed many farmers working their fields and tending their animals. I saw for the first time terrace farming in practice. It was incredible to see plots of land scaling the slope of the land. We also passed men and women carrying water and supplies on their shoulders with wooden supports. It was a very different way of life than what we had come from,"* said Donelan.

After this eye-opening section of the journey, the 40 Americans and their guide were dropped off in a tiny airport, with a terminal that did not even have enough seating for all the passengers. Another period of hanging around then ensued, and just as night was falling, the group boarded an old Soviet plane for the final – and most harrowing – leg of their trip to Xi'an.

*"It was a scary flight in the pitch black of night,"* Donelan explained. The only lights visible through the aircraft windows were those of the terminal, but sleep was not the order of the day for the exhausted passengers who had left Dallas over a day before. The aircraft that their hosts had made available to them – an Ilyushin Il-18 – was hardly conducive for them to sit back, relax and enjoy the flight. It was a twin-prop, with two propellers on each wing, and so loud that those on board could barely hear the person sitting next to them. This background noise was the soundtrack to the two-and-a-half hour flight taking the US delegation to the city of Xi'an. The Soviet craft was old, with the seats in poor repair and covered in worn fabric. The in-flight cuisine certainly did nothing to lift the travelers' spirits either. *"The crew handed out little cardboard boxes with our dinner in them,"* said Donelan, who nowadays is a professional photographer based in Florida. *"I remember a sandwich of some kind, a wedge of cheese and not much else. I can't remember if they gave us a drink or not."*

An hour and a spartan meal into the flight, the aircraft suddenly hit a patch of turbulence as a storm broke out over the dark China sky. The plane was buffeted so much that the plastic moldings on the ceiling came loose and hit passengers in the face. Water then began to seep through the fuselage due to damage caused by the storm, which somebody managed to cleverly divert onto the floor as opposed to those sitting in the seats... An hour and a half after this impromptu shower, the Soviet craft finally landed in Xi'an and the group from Texas finished off their epic journey with a bus-ride from the airport to the Shaanxi Sports Hotel which was hosting all of the teams from abroad who were taking part in the tournament. Despite travelling for over a day, the Sting Soccer Club players forced themselves through a one-hour training session after they had checked into the hotel. After all, they had a "*world championship*" to win in two weeks' time.

The competition was held from 14–26 October 1984 and featured eight teams. These included four from abroad: Rose Reilly and Elisabetta Vignotto's Italy who had won the second edition of the *Mundialito* two months earlier, Japan, Australia and the USA represented by Sting SC. The other four entries were Chinese teams, namely Shaanxi, Tianji, Guangxi and Liaoning. The eight of them were divided into two groups, with the top two qualifying for the semi-finals.

To mark the occasion, the opening match was played instead in Beijing, at the Workers' Stadium on 14 October, with Italy taking on local outfit Liaoning in Group A. It followed an opening ceremony which not all of the teams were invited to attend. It also appears (and we will touch on this later) that the Chinese Soccer Federation was so convinced that the Italians would win the tournament that they thought it a matter of course that they should play the opening match. Italy justified this decision by inflicting a 5-1 defeat on their opponents.

Over 1,000 kilometers south of the Chinese capital in the city of Xi'an, the Sting SC youngsters got their campaign under way in Group B against home team Shaanxi. In front of a packed stadium, the girls from Texas were filled with a sense of patriotism on what was a unique occasion for them. "*One thing that did stick out in my mind was the scoreboard,*" said Donelan. "*It was the first time I looked up and saw the letters 'USA' on the scoreboard. Normally when we played in the US we were called 'Sting' or 'Dallas Sting'. That's when it first struck me that we weren't playing just for our club team or our city. We weren't even playing for our state or region. We were representing our country! That made me proud and I didn't want to let my country down. I wanted to win!*" Spurred on by this sense of patriotic duty, they recorded their first win in the competition 2-0.

Despite then going on to lose to eventual group-winners Australia and draw with Tianjin, the Texans finished second in Group B and qualified for the semi-finals. In the other group, Italy and Japan made it through to the final four. The first phase of the tournament had been a success as most of the matches drew crowds of over 10,000, many of whom cycled to the stadiums, as Kinder recalled with a smile: "*There were always lots of fans at our matches and I can still see those thousands of black bikes parked in front of the stadium. We often wondered to ourselves how people knew which one was theirs!*" This was not the only amusing story that the Americans brought back with them from China. Whenever they asked for water ahead of one of their matches, the tournament officials would bring them hot water to make tea. "*No-one wanted tea, but they even gave us metal mugs to drink out of,*" Donelan grinned. "*We realized though that if we filled the mugs with hot water before kick-off and left them in the locker rooms, we'd have cold water come half-time...*" The central defender also recalled that there was no way of keeping water cold or cooling it down when it was alongside the pitch.

With matches two or three days apart, the Texans filled their spare time with training sessions, school work and excursions, most notably a visit to the famous site of the terra cotta army depicting the troops of the first emperor of China – an armada of 8,000 sculpted soldiers uncovered by chance by Chinese famers back in 1974. They were also lucky enough to see the wild goose pagoda, the drum tower, the bell tower and the ramparts in a city that was once the imperial capital of China.

Before the semi-final against Italy on 22 October, the members of the US delegation met at the bar of their hotel for drinks (soft, of course), in the hopes of raising their spirits ahead of a match against the tournament favorites. The match was played at the Xi'an Municipal Stadium where the previously placid crowd finally came to life for the first time in the tournament. *"Most of the spectators were dressed in black,"* said Donelan, *"so we could always see where our fans were as they were the only ones in colored clothing."* The US supporters in the stand were not the only ones to stand out, with the players from the Sting Soccer Club creating quite a stir by knocking out the Italians in a match that went the distance, and beyond.

After 120 minutes of normal and extra time, the two teams were locked 1-1. The resulting penalty shoot-out then took a turn for the worse for the Italians, who missed four out of five! An article published on 25 October 1984 in the Italian newspaper *La Repubblica* described it as an undeserved defeat, and indeed Italy hit the woodwork no fewer than five times. The journalist went on to add that Reilly had finished the tournament as top scorer while Viviana Bontacchio and Ettore Recagni were voted best player and best coach, even going so far as to point out that Recagni had apparently been approached to give advice to coaches from all around China, no less! Unsurprisingly, Kinder saw it all from a different angle from the Italian journalist, saying: *"The Italian team coach was over-confident for our game and I think that played to our advantage"*.

Donelan – a defender – went into more depth, saying that the Italians' style of play was too clichéd. *"Everything the Italian team did was always through Rose Reilly. Once we shut her down it was an equal game. She could not get the ball and distribute it so their attack was disrupted. They depended upon her so much that once we marked her out of the game, they could not play their game."*

The former No.7 explained that while the Italians were no doubt the better team, they seemed to be less motivated. *"I believe our youth was an advantage both physically and mentally. Physically we were in top shape and our endurance is what kept us in the game against Italy. Mentally we were not a team that was accustomed to losing. We expected to win when we played. Kinder told us we could win and that's what we did. We didn't give up and I think that frustrated the*

*Italians."*

Reilly and her team-mates nevertheless finished their campaign on a high, thrashing Japan 5-1 in the match for third place played on 23 October, after the latter had slipped to a similarly crushing defeat the day before to Australia in the second semi-final (6-2). The final therefore saw outsiders Sting SC pitted against Australia.

The two teams had already met in the group stage, with the Matildas winning by the tightest of margins. *"We were a young team and it was the first game we played after arriving in China and everything was under unusual circumstances,"* Kinder said. *"We weren't accustomed to losing and after losing that game we all took note. Probably nerves were to blame as well. For the final game we were back on track in our comfort zone wanting to redeem ourselves."*

Fired up and looking for revenge, the Dallas players headed to the Shaanxi Provincial Stadium on 24 October, and the two teams played out a hard-fought battle in front of a far-from-capacity crowd, with the USA edging it 1-0. The only goal of the game came in the 65th minute courtesy of one of the three captains of the team, Toni Catchings. And she it was who was presented the trophy by the tournament organizers – a rather curious piece of silverware sealed in a Plexiglas box. After posing with this strangest of cups, answering questions from journalists and doing a lap of honor, the young champions headed back to their hotel, only to be greeted by some bad news. While the trophy was being presented just after the victory over the Australians, Kinder *"was taken aside by the tournament officials to explain that we were not able to fly back in time to catch our return to the United States because they had not expected us to play in the final game"*. Kinder was so preoccupied by this incredible piece of news that he missed the trophy ceremony. *"Airplanes were not regularly scheduled in that part of China at that time,"* he said. *"Because we were in the final game they told us that we needed to leave immediately because we had missed our flight. We would now have to take a train to Guangzhou and then fly* to Hong Kong." Donelan recalled. *"We were their guests and we were given no itinerary, nor did we know what they had planned for us until they told us. Each day was like that. They had control over getting us back to Guangzhou. No one knows why we were not told about our travel dilemma until after our final game."* According to Kinder, the group would almost certainly have been put through a similar journey to the outbound leg had they been knocked out of the tournament earlier than expected. Instead however, they had a similarly stressful trip ahead of them.

Once the girls arrived back at the Shaanxi Sports Hotel after their win over Australia, Kinder told them to have a quick shower and pack their bags post haste. And in their hurry, the trophy got left behind... Never again would the players see the curious cup hidden away in its Plexiglas casing. They also missed the end-of-tournament festivities which were scheduled to last until 26 October.

Almost two weeks after landing in China, the US delegation found themselves having to leave the province of Shaanxi in a panic. To cap it all off, the journey ahead of them was once again set to be long and arduous. The 40 of them had to get a train from Xi'an and head north towards Beijing, where they would change and head back south to Hong Kong to catch a plane back to Dallas. That final leg by air went off without a hitch, but the train trip to Hong Kong was once again far from smooth. After travelling through the night, the train stopped in a station at 7 am. About half of the team had exited the train when suddenly it lurched forward and began moving. Some of the players were scared that they would be left behind on the platform and so jumped back on board the buffet carriage before returning to their accommodation. *"Walking through the train cars made us appreciate that they provided us with such a wonderful rail car to travel in when we witnessed what a standard rail car was for the average Chinese traveler,"* said Kinder. While they may not have managed to book the air tickets in time, the Chinese Federation at least had the good grace to send their US guests home first class. Seated in their luxury carriage, the

Texans crossed the Yangzi river and got to marvel at how Chinese workers used buffalo to help with their tasks.

After two long days on board trains, the group finally reached Hong Kong where they boarded a flight for Dallas. In total, the return journey took them two and a half days! Fortunately, the achievements of the Sting SC youngsters did not go unnoticed by the US Soccer Federation. After all, this was the first time that a US soccer team –men's or women's – had won a tournament. *"Our men's team had not had the success that my club soccer team had internationally. The women's national team was formed as a direct result of our success in Xi'an,"* said coach Kinder, before backing up his theory. *"The result was so favorable in China, the US Soccer Federation realized that there was enough talent and interest that our female soccer players could compete successfully internationally"*.

As mentioned in the chapter on the Italian *Mundialitos,* a squad of players was selected between 22 July and 4 August 1985 at a training camp in Baton Rouge, Louisiana. 17 women aged under 25 were selected to make up the first US national women's squad, but no-one from Sting SC took part in the event. In fact, none of them were aware that the camp in Baton Rouge was even taking place! Selector Mike Ryan, who had been coaching in Seattle for a large number of years, picked a team made up of players primarily from the west coast of the USA, which ruled out those from Sting SC who had been flying their country's flag around the world for a long while. Taking 1984 and 1985 as an example, Kinder's team won no fewer than seven competitions: the Robbie Tournament in Toronto; the Washington Area Girls Soccer Tournament; the Xi'an tournament in China; the Texas, Colorado and Tennessee youth soccer championships, and the Norway Cup, which was the biggest soccer tournament in the world held every year in Norway featuring anything from 1,400 to 1,700 teams of youngsters aged 10–19.

Despite their utter dominance on the national and international stages, no players or backroom staff from Sting SC were part of the first US national team that was officially created in August 1985, despite being standard-bearers for their country across the globe, and with the backing of top US soccer federation executives Don Greer and Werner Fricker. Kinder even made an official request that the US Soccer Federation recognize the Sting SC players as members of the national team, but to no avail – he never received an answer. Even today, Ryan is still seen as the first official coach of the US national team. "*That has bothered me forever,*" said Kinder, who is still hurt by the lack of recognition to this day. A cursory glance at the results achieved by Ryan's team at the *Mundialito* 1985 in Italy (where they finished last with a draw and three defeats) would also imply that the Sting Soccer Club would have made a better job of representing their country on this occasion...

It should be noted however that in 1985, Ryan picked two future winners of the first official World Cup organized by FIFA in China in 1991, namely Lori Henry and Michelle Akers. And while none of the girls who won the tournament in Xi'an were part of the group selected for the third edition of the *Mundialito* in Italy, one of them would go on to be picked at a later date, with Carla Werden Overbeck winning Olympic gold in 1996 and the World Cup with the USA in 1991 and 1999. Hardly surprisingly when you considered how well she had been coached as a youngster...

# RESULTS FROM XI'AN WOMEN'S TOURNAMENT 1984

## Group A

14 October 1984: Italy 5 - 1 Liaoning

15 October 1984: Japan 1 - 0 Guangxi

17 October 1984: Italy 6 - 0 Japan

17 October 1984: Liaoning 2 - 0 Guangxi

19 October 1984: Italy 9 - 0 Guangxi

19 October 1984: Japan 2 - 1 Lianing

## Group B

14 October 1984: Australia 3 - 1 Tianjin

14 October 1984: Shaanxi 0 - 2 Sting SC

16 October 1984: Australia 1 - 0 Sting SC

16 October 1984: Shaanxi 1 - 1 Tianjin

18 October 1984: Shaanxi 2 - 3 Australia

18 October 1984: Sting SC 0 - 0 Tianjin

## Semi-finals

22 October 1984: Sting SC 3 - 2 Italy

22 October 1984: Australia 6 - 2 Japan

## Match for seventh place

23 October 1984: Shaanxi 1 - 3 Guangxi

**Match for fifth place**

23 October 1984: Tianjin 2 - 1 Liaoning

**Match for third place**

23 October 1984: Italy 5 - 1 Japan

**Final**

24 October 1984: Sting SC 1 - 0 Australia

Source: *Mark Cruickshank - Rec. Sport Soccer Statistics Foundation*

# THE HISTORY OF THE INTERNATIONAL WOMEN'S FOOTBALL TOURNAMENT

I n the mid-1980s, the fate of women's soccer hung in the balance. Having kept a watchful but distant eye on the various 'pirate' tournaments organized throughout the previous years, FIFA was forced to recognize the interest that the sport was gaining. And yet, world soccer's governing body still only had eyes for the men's game. This fact was pointed out by Norwegian soccer federation member Ellen Wille at the 45th FIFA congress held in Mexico City on 29 May 1986.

Specifically, she deplored the complete absence of any mention of women's soccer in what was the latest FIFA annual report. *"I was very nervous because I was going to have to speak in front of 150 men,"* said Wille in an article published on the governing body's website. It turned out to be an historic speech in more ways than one since she was the first woman ever to speak at a FIFA congress, despite the fact that these gatherings had been held every year since 1904...

Former FIFA president Joseph S. Blatter recalled Wille's speech in a visit to Norway in 1999:

*I do remember Mexico City in 1986 very well. There was a*

*young woman from Norway, Ellen Wille was her name. She was small, and the table for speakers was tall, when she entered it on the FIFA Congress in Mexico City. Wille criticised us because we had not written anything about women's football in FIFA's Annual Report. I was the General Secretary at that time. President João Havelange criticised me because of that. Havelange told me: 'From now, you must remember the women's football!' That was the first time in FIFA's history that a women talked at the congress.*

The woman now known as *"the mother of Norwegian women's soccer"* in her home country did not merely point an accusatory finger at FIFA's failures in terms of women's soccer, she also asked for women to have their own World Cup and to be able to take part in the Olympic Games. President João Havelange took note of her speech and committed to supporting women's soccer, most notably by creating a commission dedicated to its development. Furthermore, the governing body also looked into running a 'trial' World Cup, as mentioned in one of the executive committee accounts:

*It is being organised and supervised directly by the Asian Football Confederation under the auspices of FIFA. The viability of a future Women's World Championship will be decided on the outcome of this tournament.*

Having already hosted any number of international women's soccer tournaments over recent years, Asia was the natural choice to hold the future competition.

Impressed by the rapid development of women's soccer in the People's Republic of China and by its ability to organize tournaments in the country, FIFA chose them to host its experimental World Cup slated for June 1988. According to *"Soccer, Women, Sexual Liberation: Kicking off a New Era,"* by Fan Hong and J.A. Mangan, the tournament was sponsored by Hong Kong billionaire Henry Fok, a businessman who was politically engaged in favor of the People's Republic of China and whom Blatter himself described as a *'Chinese patriot'*. Fok was president of the Hong Kong soccer federation and a member of the Finance Commission and Organizing Committee for the FIFA World Cup between 1978 and 1996. He received the FIFA Order of Merit in 1998, and was also vice-president of the Women's Football Commission. On his death in October 2006, shortly after Forbes magazine had ranked him as having the ninth greatest fortune in Hong Kong, FIFA recalled that *"the first FIFA Women's World Cup held in China in 1991 would surely never have seen the light of day if not for his passion for the sport"*. Unfortunately for Taiwan, they could not compete with the wealth and standing within FIFA of this local rival, and they became the forgotten players in this particular story.

Regardless of how the host nation had been selected, the trial World Cup was up and running. It was named the International Women's Football Tournament and took place in the province of Guangdong, which neighbors the administrative region of Hong Kong that was so dear to Fok's heart. And for the first time, at least one representative from each continent was invited.

# INTERNATIONAL WOMEN'S FOOTBALL TOURNAMENT

**Venue**: China

**Organized by**: The Asian Football Confederation (AFC) under the auspices of FIFA

**Date**: 1 June – 12 June 1988

After dozens of official women's tournaments played all around the world, FIFA finally authorized and oversaw an official women's soccer competition, called the International Women's Football Tournament. Although it was organized by the AFC, those at the top of the governing body attended the main matches which were played in the four Chinese cities of Guangzhou, Foshan, Jiangmen and Panyu.

In another first, the six continental confederations sent at least one representative to China. In order to promote the sport correctly, the relevant national associations decided to send their best teams. UEFA chose Sweden and Norway – the European champions from 1984 and 1987 respectively – as well as the Netherlands and Czechoslovakia. The AFC meanwhile was represented by the People's Republic of China, Thailand and Japan, who finished second in the Asian championships in 1986. The USA and Canada represented CONCACAF, Brazil CONMEBOL, Australia the OFC and Côte d'Ivoire for CAF. The overall selection was somewhat arbitrary since none of the 12 teams were required to play qualifiers for the tournament in China, but since the aim was to convince the rest of the soccer family that women were up to the task of playing their sport, the means would hopefully justify the ends...

A total of 216 players went over to Asia from 1 – 12 June 1988, and unsurprisingly given the way the countries had been chosen, the standard of play varied. Teams like Sweden and Norway had been around for 10 years, while others had been formed much more recently. This was very much the case with Canada, whose first official match had taken place as recently as 7 July 1986 against USA. *"Across such a large country, finding the financial resources to get the players together was the main issue,"* said Sylvie Béliveau who was assistant coach of the Canadian team at the Chinese tournament in 1988. *"We had regional trials followed by national selection with the best players from each province."* Brazil were not much further down the line, having played their first official match against USA at the fourth and penultimate edition of the *Mundialito* in Italy, on 22 July 1986 – 15 days after the Canadians. Côte d'Ivoire's first official match was at the tournament itself and saw them face the Netherlands. The game took place in Foshan on 1 June 1988 and was the opening match of a competition that would prove crucial for the future of women's soccer...

*"We all knew at the time that it was the first ever FIFA tournament so it was a trial run for a potential Women's World Cup,"* said former Australian player Moya Dodd on the official website of the FIFA Museum. *"We knew that we were writing a chapter of history. We were also under pressure, because this tournament was a showcase for women's soccer so that FIFA could officially organize a World Cup and give us world-renowned competitions at regular intervals."* The *Matildas* arrived in China with no real preparation behind them, and found themselves up against it from the start. The draw put them in Group B along with Norway, Brazil and Thailand. Group C comprised Sweden, Japan, USA and Czechoslovakia, while Group A brought together Côte d'Ivoire, the Netherlands, Canada and the

People's Republic of China. The host country was naturally given the honor of getting the tournament under way on 1 June 1988 in Guangzhou.

As was customary, an opening ceremony was held before the first match, at the Tianhe Sports Centre Stadium in Guangzhou. Spectators were treated to performances which included demonstrations of the traditional dance of the dragon. The only thing missing, however, was the players, as Béliveau explained: "*The teams were represented by Chinese youngsters, so while our flag was on parade, we weren't*". She pointed out that perhaps this was due to the packed fixture list. "*With three matches to play in the space of six days ahead of the quarter-finals, the organizers maybe thought that it was best not to tire us out. It's ironic that the matches were so bunched up, and yet at the same time, we were meant to go out onto the pitch and justify our status...*"

While FIFA were uncertain about the levels of some of the teams ahead of the competition, they could be sure that women's soccer would bring in the crowds. For the opening match between China and Canada, over 45,000 spectators flocked to Tianhe Stadium in Guangzhou on 1 June 1988. "*For the Canadian players it was like Daniel going into the lion's den, from six spectators to a boisterous 45,000,*" said Canucks coach Neil Turnbull to the *Edmonton Sun*. The hosts were indeed lionesses, opening the scoring in the 23rd minute via Wu Weiying. Their appetite continued into the second half, and Sun Qingmei put the match beyond doubt in the 70th minute. Canada thus slipped to a 2-0 defeat but "*could be proud of their performance*", according to their coach.

All 12 teams in the competition played their first match on the same day. The other game in Group A saw Côte d'Ivoire take on the Netherlands, with the African nation tumbling to a 3-0 defeat in their first official match. In Group B, Norway and Australia enjoyed wins over Thailand (4-0) and Brazil (1-0) respectively. There was also an absolute goal-fest for fans in Jiangmen, where USA inflicted a 5-2 defeat on Japan! Carin Jennings-Gabarra, who would go onto be a World Cup and Olympic Gold medal winner, also recorded the first ever hat-trick in the history of the US women's team. Sweden were less spectacular but every bit as efficient, squeezing past Czechoslovakia by the narrowest of margins in the second Group C match.

With 18 goals in six matches, the competition had got off to a very promising start, which was important if women's soccer was to win over the thousands of spectators in the stands at the games plus those following on TV. Of the 26 matches at the tournament, no fewer than eight were shown live on Chinese television! Plenty of interest came from the curiosity value of the nations involved – some more than others. *"The blondes got a lot of interest,"* grinned former Australian player Debbie Nichols. *There weren't any in China at the time so we got a lot of attention."* Teammate Theresa Deas was quick to confirm this. *"When we went to the zoo with the team, people followed us around. They lined up behind us rather than to see the pandas!"* In 1981, US club Sting SC had received similar treatment when they were invited to take part in the second edition of the World Women's Football Invitational Tournament in Taiwan, with former player Jody Weiss Venturoni telling the *Dallas News* website that blondes needed extra security since people in Taiwan kept trying to touch their heads, believe it or not...

The Canadian team were housed in the luxurious White Swan Hotel in Guangzhou, and made the most of their days off between matches to discover what was a totally new culture to them. Their physio Gail Amort Larson recalled Chinese women sweeping the streets with brooms, as well as the military escorts that all teams in the competition were given– similar to the treatment afforded to Stade de Reims in Taipei in 1978. Béliveau meanwhile had not forgotten the flora and fauna, tai-chi lessons that they were given and then the new cuisine.

*"We wanted to be careful so we only drank water and tea all the time,"* she explained. *"I wanted a change and it was the first time in my life*

*that I drank coffee."* Both women also remembered time spent enjoying a cup of tea alongside the pitch.

Such moments of respite were all too brief, however, with matches coming thick and fast. They ran over 80 minutes and were programmed every two days. And back in 1988, they were all refereed by men – indeed it was not until the following year that the Norwegian soccer federation organized a first training course for female officials in conjunction with FIFA. This initiative paid dividends very soon: in 1991, six women officiated as assistant referees at the first official World Cup. Despite this, it was not until 1999 that women's World Cups were solely refereed by women.

After the fast and furious group stage, the top six teams along with the two best third-placed countries qualified for the quarter-finals. Unsurprisingly, Sweden and Norway would go on to make it to the final of the tournament.

The showdown for the trophy was played 12 June at the Tianhe Stadium in Guangzhou on front of 35,000 spectators. It got under way at midday, with experienced Brazilian referee Romualdo Arppi Filho in charge, two years after he had overseen the final of the men's World Cup between Argentina and West Germany. Despite having legendary player (and later coach) Pia Sundhage in their ranks, Sweden fell to a 1-0 defeat to their local rivals, just as they had in the final of Euro 1987. The only goal of the game came in the 58th minute from Linda Medalen, who would go on to win 152 caps for Norway and hoist the World Cup aloft in 1995. In the third place play-off, Brazil defeated China 4-3 on penalties after a goalless draw. The *Seleção* also had the tournament's top scorer, Lucilene Souza Marinho, who found the back of the net four times.

At the end of the day, players, organizers and spectators all agreed that the tournament had been a success. Across the 26 matches, there was a total of 81 goals at an average of just over three per match. 360,000 spectators filled the various stadia, while 200 million viewers watched the eight matches that were shown live. In the report it submitted to FIFA after the competition, the AFC stated that the tournament was proof that women's soccer henceforth deserved recognition on the world stage, going on to suggest that FIFA organize a first official global tournament in the years to come. Soccer's governing body shared the AFC's opinion, and just 18 days after the final whistle of that tournament, confirmed that there would indeed be an inaugural World Cup. The book 'FIFA 1904 – 2004: a century of football' even includes the following line on the subject: *"The president of the Swiss federation was so impressed* (by what he saw at the tournament) *that he toyed with the idea of putting President Havelange forward for the Nobel Peace Prize."* And rather incredibly, he did just that in 1988! An ironic turn of events when one considers that women had to wait decades for FIFA to deign to show their version of the sport any interest whatsoever. For those concerned about the 'result', the Nobel Peace Prize for 1988 was ultimately awarded to the United Nations peace-keeping forces...

This first FIFA-supervised tournament was of course far from flawless. The standard of the different teams in the competition was certainly not balanced, but that could be said of many events since then, including the Women's World Cup 2019 in France. In the official report on the 1991 World Cup in China, FIFA also underlined the lack of fitness of the teams at the 1988 tournament. *"The intensity of matches has increased* (compared with 1988). *Great progress has been made, especially by the European teams. Top teams can now keep up a high tempo for the full 80 minutes, which was not the case in 1988. At that time, there were many teams whose players had serious fitness problems towards the end of a game."*

This issue had been resolved in the space of a few years, as illustrated by FIFA's decision to extend women's matches from the 1995 World Cup in Sweden, which were played over the full 90 minutes, just like the men's. Finally, it was a level playing field.

# RESULTS FROM THE INTERNATIONAL WOMEN'S FOOTBALL TOURNAMENT

## Group A

1 June 1988: China 2 - 0 Canada

1 June 1988: Netherlands 3 – 0 Côte d'Ivoire

3 June 1988: China 1 - 0 Netherlands

3 June 1988: Canada 6 - 0 Côte d'Ivoire

5 June 1988: Canada 1 - 1 Netherlands

5 June 1988: China 8 - 1 Côte d'Ivoire


## Group B

1 June 1988: Norway 4 - 0 Thailand

1 June 1988: Austrlia 1 - 0 Brazil

3 June 1988: Brazil 2 - 1 Norway
3 June 1988: Australia 3 - 0 Thailand
5 June 1988: Norway 3 - 0 Australia
5 June 1988: Brazil 9 - 0 Thailand

## Group C

1 June 1988: USA 5 - 2 Japan

1 June 1988: Sweden 1 - 0 Czechoslovakia

3 June 1988: Sweden 1 - 1 USA

3 June 1988: Czechoslovakia 2 - 1 Japan

5 June 1988: Czechoslovakia 0 - 0 USA

5 June 1988: Sweden 3 - 0 Japan

## Quarter-finals

8 June 1988: China 7 - 0 Australia

8 June 1988: Sweden 1 - 0 Canada

8 June 1988: Brazil 2 - 1 Netherlands

8 June 1988: Norway 1 - 0 USA

## Semi-finals

10 June 1988: Norway 2 - 1 Brazil

10 June 1988: Sweden 2 - 1 China

## Match for third place

12 June 1988: Brazil 0 - 0 China (Brazil win 4–3 on penalties)

## Final

12 June 1988: Norway 1 - 0 Sweden

**Team of the tournament as chosen by the Chinese media:**

Elisabeth Leidinge (Sweden),

Liv Strædet (Norway), Marie Karlsson (Sweden), Heidi Støre (Norway), Eva Zeikfalvy (Sweden),

Roseli de Belo (Brazil), Linda Medalen (Norway), Carin Jennings (USA), Sun Qingmei (China),

Lucilene Souza Marinho 'Cebola' (Brazil), Ellen Scheel (Norway).

Source: *Tom Lewis - Rec. Sport Soccer Statistics Foundation*

# PHOTOS

*Mundial* 1971 – Denmark captain Lis Westberg

*Mundial 1971 - Susanne Augustesen with her parents and the trophy*

*Mundial 1971 – The Denmark team*

*WWFIT 1978 - Renée Delahaye with the Finland captain*

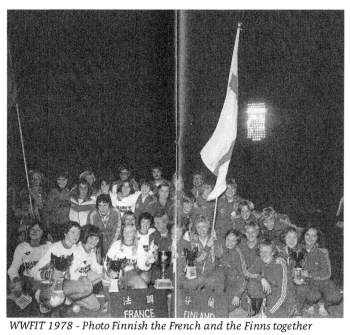

*WWFIT 1978 - Photo Finnish the French and the Finns together*

*Mundialito 1981 (Japan)- Italy's Elisabetta Vignotto with the trophy*

*Sticker depicting Pallina, the mascot of the 1984 Mundialito*

*Xi'an Tournament 1984 – USA's Sting Soccer Club*

*Xi'an Tournament: Tina Edgar and Erin Adamson after her
decisive penalty in the shoot-out win over the Italians*

*Xi'an Tournament: Sting SC captain Toni Catchings is awarded the trophy*

*Xi'an Tournament: Alicia Tannery Donelan (left)*
*with Italy's Carolina Morace*

*International Women's Football Tournament 1988: Gail Amort Larson and Dr. John Bennett (Canada)*

*IWFT: Local youngsters parading instead of the teams*

*IWFT: The tournament mascot*

# ACKNOWLEDGEMENTS

My thanks first and foremost go to those who were gracious enough to take the time to speak with me when I was researching this book. Anne Noë, Feriana Ferraguzzi, Susanne Augustesen, Sylvie Beliveau, Gail Amort Larson, Alicia Tannery Donelan and Bill Kinder– I am incredibly grateful to you all.

I would also like to thank Danish journalist Hans Krabbe who was of great help to me as I sought to get in touch with Susanne Augustesen. I would have loved to have read his book "*Den Glemte Triumph*" devoted to the 1971 tournament in Mexico, but the Danish language has never been one of my strong points...

An acknowledgement of a very special kind to Oicem Saidoun, my guru when it comes to journalism. He it was who, one day during a phone call, gave me the idea of producing a book on the history of women's soccer. No doubt he will not recollect that conversation as it then took me five years to write it – once again, better late than never...

And last but not least many thanks to Drew Lilley who translated this book from first to last, finishing off with this final acknowledgement!

# CONTENTS

WOMEN'S SOCCER: THE OFFICIAL HISTORY OF THE UNOFFICIAL WORLD CUPS   1

FOREWORD   2

HISTORY OF THE COPPA DEL MONDO OR MUNDIAL   4

MUNDIAL 1971   10

RESULTS FROM THE MUNDIAL 1971   21

THE history of the WORLD WOMEN'S FOOTBALL INVITATIONAL TOURNAMENT   23

WORLD WOMEN'S FOOTBALL INVITATIONAL TOURNAMENT 1978   27

RESULTS FROM WORLD WOMEN'S FOOTBALL INVITATIONAL TOURNAMENT 1978   32

THE HISTORY OF THE MUNDIALITO   35

MUNDIALITO 1984   39

THE HISTORY OF THE TOURNAMENTS IN THE REPUBLIC OF CHINA   45

XI'AN WOMEN'S TOURNAMENT   49

RESULTS FROM XI'AN WOMEN'S TOURNAMENT 1984   61

THE HISTORY OF THE INTERNATIONAL WOMEN'S FOOTBALL TOURNAMENT   63

INTERNATIONAL WOMEN'S FOOTBALL TOURNAMENT   67

RESULTS FROM THE INTERNATIONAL WOMEN'S   73

FOOTBALL TOURNAMENT

PHOTOS                                              76

Acknowledgements                                    84

Sources                                             87

# SOURCES

Castaing Michel. « *La "footballeuse", dernière-née des sportives a fait son entrée européenne à Turin* ». Le Monde. 5 November 1969

Pieper Lindsay. "The Beleaguered History of the Women's World Cup". Us Sport History. 2 July 2015

Pujol Ayelén. *"El dia que Argentina jugo su primer Mundial de futbol femenino»*. Pagina 12. 12 May 2018

Belkis Martinez. "*La mujer que le hizo 4 goles a Inglaterra en el estadio Azteca antes de la Mano de Dios de Maradona*". La Nacion. 6 February 2019.

Erik Garin. "Mundial (Women) 1971". rsssf.com. 29 February 2004

"Soccer goes sexy south of border". New-York Times. 27 June 1971.

Xavier Breuil. "Histoire du football féminin en Europe de la Grande Guerre jusqu'à nos jours".

Bill Wilson. "Mexico 1971 : When women's football hit the big time". BBC. 7 December 2018

Miguel Angel Garnica. "*El mundial femenil que México olvido*". El Universal. 8 March 2017

"Augustesen Susanne". Lazio Wiki

Mayse Njor. "*Da kvinderne vandt VM-guld: Sammenbrud i ørkenen, forsvundne trøjer og en 15-årigs hattrick i finalen*". berlingske.dk - 6 August 2017

Karina Jorge. "*Las unicas subcampeonas de futbol que ha tenido México*". Uno TV. 16 June 2018.

Nikoline Vestergaard. "*Verdensmester som 15-årig*" B.T. - 10 September 2007.

"*Foot féminin : Lyon écrase le PSG, record d'affluence en France*". Europe 1 - 13 April 2019

*"La Coupe du Monde de Football Féminin, les premiers tirs..."* CCT Belfort - 17 November 2015

Mark Cruickshank. "Women's World Invitation Tournament - Overview". Rec. Sport Soccer Statistics Foundation - 31 December 2009

Mark Cruickshank. "Women's World Invitation Tournament 1978". Rec. Sport Soccer Statistics Foundation - 4 June 2015

"AFC Women's Asian Cup". Wikipedia

Dave Litterer. "USA - Women - Internationals Results". Rec. Sport Soccer Statistics Foundation.

*"Mundialito 1984"*. Wikipedia

Walter Pettinati. *"MUNDIALITO 84': IL VIDEO INTEGRALE DI ITALIA - GERMANIA SU CALCIODONNE"*. calciodonne.it - 25 January 2012

Emmanuela Audisio. "Que gol di Betty profuma di mundial". La Repubblica. 28 August 1984.

*"Mundialito, le Azzurre in finale"*. La Repubblica. 26 August 1984.

Brad Townsend. "Where it all started". interactives.dallasnews.com - 3 July 2015

"About Sting". stingsoccerclub.com

"Reilly righlty at home in Hall of Fame". heraldscotland.com - 12 November 2007

*"Ellen Wille, la mère du football féminin"*. fifa.com - 30 June 2011

"Matildas 30th anniversary - FIFA women's invitation tournament 1988". youtube.com - WeAreTeam11 - 2 August 2018

*"Quand le foot fête les femmes"*. fifa.com - 8 March 2012

*"Countdown : Nur noch 88 Tage"*. fifa.com - 10 March 2015

FIFA, Christiane Eisenberg, Pierre Lanfranchi, Tony Maon et Alfred Wahl. *"FIFA 1904 - 2004: le siècle du football"*. Edition Le Cherche-Midi. April 2004

"USA lay down a marker" fifa.com - 4 March 2010

Fan Hong et J. A. Mangan. "Soccer, Women, Sexual Liberation: Kicking off a New Era". Routledge édition. 23 November 2004.